Fields of His Heart

Poems by

Wayne H. Swanger

The Watershed Journal Literary Group

The publication of this book has been partially funded by a grant from Clarion University.

ISBN 978-1-59539-060-8

Cover artwork by Susan Jayne Hadden

Used by permission

The Watershed Journal Literary Group

108 Main Street

Brookville, PA 15825

For Mary

Foreword

The first thing you should know about Wayne is that he's a gardener, a grower, raised in a community of farmers and laborers. He lives close to the land, as so many of these poems attest. He gives us the landscapes of central and northwestern Pennsylvania--barns, runs, forest floor—and in them uncovers quiet moments of insight and humor. Insight and humor mark his poems of the spirit as well. Non-doctrinaire, they instead invite us into sacred spaces of the everyday.

And the people! This collection is well-populated with workers, dreamers, lovers. Some may be hurt by the world, but they remain radiant in their humanity. Grief and joy dance here.

Whether short and aphoristic or careful and meditative, all the poems sing in conversational free verse.

Join this poet as he invites you to "share a gardener's contentment / with that which blesses / one's senses / and soul."

— Deborah Sarbin

Table of Contents

Helix

They give. I can only receive
From their hands never touched--
My benefactors, faces framed
On plaster walls or in photographs
Exhumed from attic and cellar.

Their bodies scattered
On Pennsylvania hillsides,
Under headstones as hard
As the lives they lived.

Today, I walk among them,
Names faded on grey granite:
Cover, Kendall, Cook,
Turn, Watson, Illingworth…

They give, even now,
Unknown and unknowingly.

Rows

On my side of the fence is a garden
With rows…well, sort of rows…

Widths and lengths vary,
Never straight. At night plants escape,
Seeking space in open walkways
Avoiding foot and hoe. They do no harm
In their beauty and desire
To seek sunshine and adventure.
In the light of day I let them be
Where they are; it humors me.

When foolish,
I try to arrange them
In some creative manner,
But when I'm preoccupied or sleeping
They find preferred places,
Ignoring my plan:

Columbine jumps the fence,
Sweet peas among the herbs,
Mint under the gooseberries.

On my side of the fence is a garden
With rows…well, sort of rows…

Jubilee

Flee to the south come fall,
Abandon the nest, neighbor and all.

Sprawled on a bed of disaster,
Awakened by the unfamiliar,
Alert now, he listens closely
Hearing only a truncated echo:

> *Flee to the south!*
> *Flee to the south!*
> *Flee to the south!*

The disembodied voice, a welcome relief
From nightmares of helicopter
Gunships, gaping wounds, bodies
Stacked as cordwood, collages of death
And destruction that had awakened him for years,

And more recently,
Night terrors of his life's reality:
Love lost, locked doors, filth, emptiness
And madness staring back from the bathroom mirror.

Court documents served as benchmarks
Along his path of self-destruction:

  --Divorce papers
      --Protection from Abuse Order
            --Involuntary commitment

The voice an answered prayer, although
Not his, for he had not yet learned to pray.
Staring into the abyss, considering the unthinkable,
He obeyed,

    Flee to the south!

The Tennessee sun cauterized his rage as he labored
Among Hutterite and Friend in the southern high bush,
Cultivating berries with twine and pruners in hand.
He struggled in the fields of his heart to tame the unruly,
Thin the strangled, tangled growth, and prune the dead from the
living.

His sweat a sweet unction for gall and malice.
Over time, knowing forgiveness in the fragrance of blueberries.

Quaker Meeting: A Preparatory Ritual

Bread cooling

Chicken in oven

Slaw tossed

Halva and apples sliced

Fresh bouquet cut

House quiet

Quiet as a church

Soon Friends will arrive

Then Silence

Present

This moment lives,
Born of the urschleim
Of yesterdays,
Becoming the inception
Of tomorrow's possibilities,
Unnoticed as the last breath,
As consequential
As the next heartbeat,
Ephemeral,
Yet eternal.

Choice

He bows, taps the crown of his head,
The split between Heaven and Earth.

A puzzling declaration given the object,
A fresh scar, discolored,
Ripped into his cranium a few days prior:
Raw ugliness, now morphed
Into a macabre montage
Of sutures, bristles, flesh,
Like a grotesque caterpillar
That stretches ear to ear.

They messed up my part!
(Grin turns to grimace)

Eyes welling, he gulps,
Places his hand on his throat,
Mumbles something about tubes and swelling,
Other masses, more chemo, radiation and…

The irony of choosing this over heaven.

Two Mile Run

Wade expectantly, warily
Into Two Mile's cluttered current;
A phantasmagoria
Of backyard refuse,
Collective camouflage
Guarding this trout trove
In the Pennsylvania Wilds.

Carefully scan the flotsam,
Set your jaw firmly,
Cautiously venture into the flow,
A confluence of fear and enchantment—

Be leery of rusty nail,
Glass shard, ragged steel,
Be allured by the water's clarity,
Deep undercuts, the dark, swift troughs,
Promises of abundant scale and fin.

Before mist rises…
Creel filled, spell cast,
Transfiguration complete.
You too will worship Two Mile,
Gift from God and neglect.

Final March

This is not
one of the marches
we've taken before
and we all know
there will be none
after.

Music once vivace,
then,
desperately brash,
now muted.

Silence approaches.

Cadence succumbs
to staggers.

The finish
unrecognized
until passing.

Feeding Geese

Who would not smile
At such grace …

As she casts grain
Among the geese,
Gently admonishing
The greedy ones
In perfect tones

The Rowboat
     (For Susan)

Reach out, draw in.
Reach out, draw in.
Reach out, draw in.

The cadence spoken softly, firmly;
Wide-eyed, attentive--the child listens.
She sits facing her father,
Her hands covered by his,
Oars lift and drop,
Hover and pull as required;
With voice and touch he gently,
Skillfully proffers rudiments of rowing.

In time his hands lift from hers,
She reaches and draws
Following her own cadence,
Charting her own journey,
Leaving him for a time
In her wake.

The boat adrift,
She found it years later
Abandoned on a sandy lot...

Neglected and damaged,
It spoke to her condition.

Bent by her resolve,
She mends the boat.
His work, now, her work.

Through its lines,
Dimensions, construction,
She grows to know
His pragmatism,
Precision, and passion...

Unaware her application
Of resin, paint, and patch
Heals both boat and soul.

Mistaken

I thought
It was the cat purring

It was my soul comforted

In the presence
Of God

Vigil

Amazing how quiet
A Great Pyrenees can be
When death approaches:

Her lumbering tread imperceptible
But for the barely audible sound
Of untrimmed nails on wooden floor.
She moves sparingly, instinctively
To find a vantage point,
When satisfied, heaves a heavy sigh
As she heaps herself into a white
Mound of fur and faithfulness.
This steadfast sentinel
Holds vigil by a bedside.

Listening this night,
The Great Pyrenees hears
But is not stirred
By the clock's constant cadence,
Calibration of a life passing.
She does not stir
When the clarion of bleating ewes
Arises from the barn below.
Nor does she stir when he stirs,

His breathing labored, rhythmic,
Marked by staccato exclamations
As he struggles to reach the finish.

Amazing how loud
A Great Pyrenees can be
When breathing ceases
And death departs:

A doleful bark, thunderous,
Echoes through the house,
Awakening everyone
but the dead.

Embrace

Do you remember?

I recall it vividly…
As this autumn moon
In cloudless sky.

Tea Party

Child of Light
Wracked by laughter,
Manic demons
In white bonnets
And grey dresses.

She offers suffering,
Granola bars and iced tea
While reading poetry
From places too dark
To be understood…

Only felt.

Winter Dance

Slow dance in snowshoes

On a windswept mountaintop

Ten degrees   snowing

Unforgettably frozen

In time   and their memories

Lincoln Highway Revisited: A Drive with Dad

I drove this road a good bit,
Delivered ice cream and mix
Twice a week: Monday, Friday.
First, Mercersburg, then St. Thomas,
Final stop, Chambersburg.
Left at three in the morning,
Home by eleven. Next morning,
Do it all over again…

Sheaves in the field. Look!
Must be Amish.
As a kid I fed sheaves into a thresher.
Mercy! Oat chaff is nasty, itchy stuff…

I delivered to this farmer--
Yep, a farm with a freezer in the barn.
Hard to believe I filled it
With ice cream twice a week!
Sure treated their help good,
Imagine, ice cream after the barn work!
Nope, it wasn't this farm, it was that one there…

On the top of this mountain
I rolled the truck 'cause the shoulder
Was soft. Backed up, and over it went.

Hurt my ankle when my foot got stuck
'Neath the brake pedal.
Had to climb out the window,
Could hardly walk. Funny,
I had to climb back in 'cause
I had left the truck running.
Finally, state trooper showed up.
He wanted an ambulance.
I told him nope,
First got to get the truck out.
Needed a big wrecker,
But I saved the load...
Thank Goodness
I was hauling mix that day...

Ground hog! Darn!
You hit it good--
Was in the middle of the road,
Didn't you see it?
Was already dead.
Can't believe you didn't see it...

The statie stayed all day.
Remember I had to pee so bad
Thought I'd wet the gurney.
He took me to the john.
Nice guy.
His wife was a nurse...

Big old Luke Cramer drove
The route with me a couple weeks.
He told me, "It's a helluva drive.
I wouldn't do it."
Old Luke was plain spoken,
Every sentence a swear...

Now get in the left lane
And take Route 11 to Green Village
Then right to Scotland.
Okay then. Go ahead.
Take the interstate
If you want...

Sonny died in one of these houses,
I think that one there...
No, it's this one, over there.
I remember the round porch.
Yes, that's it...

Wanted to get there in time.
Really tried, but you know...the load.
Parked the empty truck right over there,
Knew he had died before I got there.
Funny, but just felt a change pass over me.

Twilight

Beyond his twilight
Dusk envelops Dad
Apparent in his trembling hand
Unkempt appearance
Confused expression
Only the penumbra that
Portends greater darkness

A foreshadowing
Of finality
After senses and hopes
Are extinguished
One by one by one
Like candles
On a Tenebrae hearse

Burr Oak

I long to embrace
This ancient burr oak
Until its deeply wrinkled bark
Is mirrored by my body
And soul

Elegy for a Poet, Teacher, Friend

(In Memory of Alfred T. Kisubi)

I wait for words to dance once more--
A foolish fantasy, for I know
The dance ended when
His heart ceased beating,
Silenced,
Like a drumhead broken by cumulated

Loss,
    Cruelty,
        Blood,
            Exile

Now, I pick up his pen,
Uncomfortable, I feel its weight.
Unbalanced in my hand
It recognizes unworthiness--
It will no longer dance
To his music.

His pen I now bear,

Knowing in skilled hand

It moved like a dancer on stage--

Glide,

     Leap,

          Turn,

               Bend,

                    Stretch,

A word-dance choreographed

To the music of his soul,

Tableau of line and sound.

Now, in my hand,

Like a child's first steps...

               It totters and stumbles.

Mary

Your essence
Like jasmine
Causes passersby
To stop
Breathe deeply

World turns
To sweetness

Sorrow ends

Risk

We covertly planned
to invade Afghanistan and Iraq,
a strategy to win the game.
Success was ours, secured
by our bold, reckless collusion.
However, victory was lost
by a mother's declaration
that supper would not wait
...*a cold one not worth eating.*

We cleared the pieces
and smiled with youthful certitude;
The board would be reset tomorrow
so we might laugh, bluster
and plot again.

We did not know then
the Voices planned to invade
your head and tell you things
only you could hear.
They would become your only friends,
when your old ones were outed
as agents, CIA operatives
that eavesdropped--

                everywhere.

Now you sit alone, vigilant,

in the corner, wide eyes darting,

lights out, shades drawn.

Fearful. Silent.

Knowing others plot,

and await your surrender.

The Milking

Leaning in deep,

With ease he assumes his work

As one might put on a suit of clothes:

      Casually, unconsciously, capably.

Adjusting the stool

He presses his head to the Ayrshire's flank,

Reaches beneath her bovine bulk,

Seizes two teats

Suspended from her swollen udder

And commences the symbiotic ritual

Performed in this old barn

For generations.

The galvanized pail

Set below her hindquarters

And between his knees

Fills steadily

As his sinewy hands, powerful and sure,

Pump like pistons.

The muffled murmur of flowing milk

Soothes milker and milked alike;

Eyes open and close languidly

As they relieve one another of their burdens.

Clarion River

i

Blue Heron silhouetted
Against riverbank

It stalks in silence

ii

Eagle perched above

Surveys with yellow eyes
A silent kayaker below

iii

Morning mist shrouds
River and heart…

By day's end
It will lift
From only one

A Cautionary Note

In their grabby, greasy hands
The promisors
Bear torches
Of the coming inferno,
Conflagration lit by this note
Of servitude
Advertised as a ticket
To all that you dreamed of--

Exotic places, wheels, wardrobe,
Your own bed and breakfast
Carefree, effortless,
Simply sign the dotted line
Of your demise.

Indentured, you will never own
But lease your life,
Your soul bound by fear
Of losing what you never had
Stalking you like a big cat,
It leaps and forecloses
Apparent then that leverage
Was illusory,
The fulcrum positioned
By grabby, greasy hands

The principle remains
The same:
After years of paying
You will have nothing…

         But empty hands.

A Pastoral

(In Memory of John and Anne Turn)

Slow hum of a few notes,
His internal metronome
Weds cadence to movement.

Labor the motif,
Each task a song;
Their farm blessed
By the music.

Tendrils creeping up walls
Of their fieldstone home,
Clinging and inching
Year by year.

Inside, she too hums…
A counterpoint.

Together, harmonious
Melody, motet
For no one
But themselves.

Color and water
Indistinguishable,

Gray as scattered ashes--
Rain and mist linger
Over fallow fields.

Barn and house now
Silent.

Their music echoes
In the distance.

Garden Pleasures

Come into our garden.

Poke your nose into a vortex of petals.

Breathe.

Delight in fragrances subtle, sweet, bold.

Listen to blossoms. Hear

Music of evening rains,

Morning birdsong, humming bees.

Kneel with me,

Share a gardener's contentment

In that which blesses

One's senses

And soul.

Sunset

Lowering sun softens
The landscape of decrepitude;
Shadows lengthen
Obscuring the clutter
Of dependency.
The hourglass empties
Of days filled
With game shows,
Medications,
Cajoling and admonishments,
Endless appointments,
Bedpans, whimpers,
Frustration, rage
And eventually…
        surrender.

Outed

Oh! Are you really one of those?
I hear it still. I stood naked,
My cloak of obfuscation
Dropped and rumpled
Around my ankles.

For two years,
A surreptitious identity
Was hidden by a calculus
Of concealment.
My identity reviled
But not revealed
Until that morning.

A winter morning,
Cold and brittle,
Our shovels
Kept a rasping rhythm
As we labored together
Elbow to elbow;
Family news, banter, laughter
Filled the air.
Perhaps, his was a suspicious nature
Like Holmes, Javert, Poiret, Gamache.
Or perhaps, Fate interposed.

Nonetheless, conversation
Took the inevitable turn:

He asked, *Where you from?*
        I replied, *Pennsylvania.*

His questions, my answers…

How long you been here?
        Couple of years.

What brought you here?
        Work.

Where do you work?
(I winced at his doggedness.)
        In town.

What do you do?
        Teach.

Now, finally, unavoidably,
The coup de grace--

Where do you teach?
        The University.

He leaned on his shovel,
Stared in my direction,
Eyebrows arched,
Shook his head,
Spluttered, *Oh,*
Are you really one of those?

Shoveling finished,
Winter ended…

But the coldness never did.

Pray

Warm luminescence
On the forest floor
Will, in time,
Fill the grave
Emptiness
Left hanging
And twitching
In this darkness.

In endless silence
Constrictive pleas
Echo loudly
Profound and unheard.

For now,
His absence,
A taut noose,
Suffocating hearts
Of family and friends.

Solace

Occasionally, in the midst
Of tragedy and distress
We enter the silence.

Stillness whispers:

      All will be well.

Arrhythmic

She lost her rhythm,
Grown weary
Of the effort,
Age the culprit--
Her once perfect ear,
Pilfered, nearly gone.

Choices few
For an aged arrhythmic
Trapped
As the orchestra plays on--
The rhythm escapes her.

In a measure,
Or two,
Bewildered,
She lays down
Her instrument,
Abandons the stage.

Advice

(Thanks to Tim O'Brien)

Intention may guide,
But must not insist,

Good advice for writing,
As well as love.

Minding Death

The mind just hasn't gotten used to
Her falling away, unnoticed
At first, insidious, relentless,
Eyes once bright with life
Fading slowly to dull vacancy.

The mind just hasn't gotten used to
This rending of spirit from flesh
Punctuated by strangled breath silenced,
An ebbing pulse quieted,
Her body still--

         Death,

            Finality.

The mind just hasn't gotten used to
The unctuous comforters who rush in
Like wind through an open door
Offer platitudes and scripture--
Nonsensical patter:

     The end of suffering.

       Better places.

          Heavenly reunions.

Before the body is washed and bagged
Before those left behind feel their loss
And can hold on briefly... ever so gently.

The mind just hasn't gotten used to
These merchants of death,
Intruders in polished wingtips
Who offer their finest
For the loved one lost
And assurance the array
Of custom caskets
Made of expensive alloys
And polished woods
Will reflect your devotion
And the luster of the grave
Resting place of the beloved.

The mind hasn't gotten used to
This assemblage of the bereaved
Gathered to mourn the deceased
In unison, in traditions of gladioli
And "Rock of Ages" sung as slowly
As her last breaths,
The rattle in our throats
A tribute to the finely tuned
Machinery of processions,
Hearses for hire, and backhoes.

The mind hasn't gotten used to
Standing by the graveside
Looking into the abyss
Dug with remains
Of an insurance policy
Bought to gift grandchildren.
We recognize our poverty,
Bankrupt of gratitude, stingy
With our attention until now.

The mind just hasn't gotten used to
This falling away of loved ones,
Echoes and memories remain;
No future, no present; only
The past once sown in love and laughter
Harvested in liquor and loneliness.

The mind just hasn't gotten used to
This shock of loss morphed
Into a malaise of suppressed tears,
Unanticipated memories,
Interrupted thoughts stumbling
Vacantly through the day.

The mind just hasn't gotten used to
This mourning when her son rises
To find darkness persists;
Dawn arrested by the grave notion
That the giver of his life has lost hers.

The mind just hasn't gotten used to
This bedside epiphany:
She, at seventeen,
A child herself,
Loved her child,
As only a child could.
Now, her child holds her hand,
As she, like a child, returns home.

Shrug

Where is the next porcupine?
The question elicits laughter,
Or, occasionally, uncomfortable silence.
Yet, it is a worthy question,
For each encounter
With the porcine rodent
Pricks curiosity and provides insight.
It can be a pleasant encounter,
Or not.

A porcupine schlumps about
In its whereabouts,
Unhurried and unconcerned.
It makes no claim to property,
Insists on only one right--
The right to be left alone.

It will not approach others,
Let alone aggress,
For all purposes, a pacifist.
Yet, when attacked
By dog or man
Its defense is neither fangs

Nor claws, but a nonchalant

Shrug of the shoulders

That confidently suggests...

If you must.

Compassion: A Missed Opportunity

The old man holding a cardboard sign
stapled to two pieces of wood
stood on the periphery of the crowd.
His body tensed as he strained to keep the sign aloft.
Staring straight ahead he spoke to no one
as if he could get the speaker's attention by resolve alone.
The man moved to the center of the crowd
and held the sign in front of the speaker
who gave no indication of notice.
He slowly turned around and the crowd read
this message written in a coarse hand:

I trust my life
and the lives of my two marine sons
in the hands of the President.
God bless America.

I, who believe his trust given to the untrustworthy,
and his faith rested on the shifting sands of politics,
felt pity for this father of two beloved sons.

Today, just a day later,
I regret not following the old man as he left the crowd.
I might have offered him my hand
and bought him a cup of coffee.

I could have asked him his sons' names

and where they are stationed,

smiled, nodded, and said that he must be proud of his boys.

I should have wished them both peace and God's protection.

Wren

Jenny wren scolds
As I approach
The clothespin bag
Hanging on the line
Since last autumn

Her loved ones
Ever so snug
In a muslin nest
I was too lazy
To put away

Sanctuary

My garden
Is a sanctuary: A balm
For those needing succor,
A respite from electronic bytes,
Images and sounds
That irritate and subdue the senses.
Escape from solicitations for things
That are bought at a cost
Greater than money.
Leave your shoes by the gate.
Knead the soil with your toes.
Pray. Let your roots run deep
In this place of solitude and solace,
Coition of soil, seed and sweat.
Breathe deeply of buzzing silence.
Unclench your heart and hands,
Gather blooms if you'd like.
Wrap your mind around a bouquet
Of love's work and time well spent.
Stay in my garden as long as you need,
Or, until this place is no longer mine alone,
But rather ours to work, to enjoy,
To offer to others who
Seek such a place.

Leave Taking

Quips and beer at an outdoor café,
The sun brilliant and alive.
Occasionally, we lean forward,
Look at one another intently,
Throw our heads back and laugh
As if there's no tomorrow.

I was bemused to see us so,
That is, as we had never been
When we breathed the same air
And labored passionately with polemics
Honed fine and sharp, wielded as weapons
In our academic arena. When not in battle,
Only perfunctoriness passed between us.

Then, his lungs clouded and our hearts
Softened in new knowledge
Of uncertainty,
Struggle,
Alternative treatments,
Reconciliation,
Mortality.

How long would the dream have lasted
Had I not asked him,

Do you know you are on the other side?

He lowered his glass,
His eyes widened, face puckered,
He sobbed and vanished.

Gardenia

White as yesterday's clouds
Fragrant as an early spring morning
Not aware of its own beauty
Why does it induce melancholy

Transcendence

> *(For Rebekah)*

Spirit wind
Skips across the waters,
Swings open the gate,
Touches her soul,
  An aeolian harp.
Knowing the Divine Companion
As did Lawrence, Francis, Rumi.
She is kin to all.

No time for dogma, creeds,
Articles of faith.
No need for
Exegesis, polemics,
Ponderous lexicons…

For in the knowing
She need not understand.

Lessons at Carlisle Indian Industrial School (1879-1918)

Lesson 1:

Oblivious, Little Bear sat,
A front row seat,
Dead center,
While Black Robe wielded
His chalk stone like a saber,
Slashing violently
Letters on the slate.
Many flinched,
The youngest cried,
Little Bear sat stone-faced,
No different than he looks
In this old photograph.

Lesson 2:

Oblivious to Little Bear,
Black Robe wielded
His chalk stone
Like a knife cruelly carving
Words on the slate.
Letters white, exact, uniform,
Exemplars for the unsaved

Mourners with shorn heads
And leather-shod feet:

BOUNCE
POUNCE
TROUNCE

Look! Rhyming words!
Do you hear the music
Of your new language?
Say them!

Little Bear remained mute,
Preferring the music of the old:

LAKOTA
DAKOTA
NAKOTA

He chanted this music
Deep within
So Black Robe would not beat
A steady rhythm
On his back
Once again.

Lesson 3:

Oblivious to Little Bear,
Black Robe pulled
His chalk stone
From his pocket like a gun
And banged on the slate.

These rhyming words
Are verbs. Action words!
Read them!

BOUNCE
POUNCE
TROUNCE

Little Bear did not read.
He knew these things.
Coyote, big cat and fox
Had taught him just
As Sitting Bull had shown
Yellow Hair and his soldiers
At Little Big Horn.

Lesson 4:

Oblivious to Little Bear,
Black Robe became a soldier
Of a different sort.
His weapons were scissors,
Leather boots, textbooks,
Discipline and education.
He sought to kill the Indian
And save the Man.
The tally?
One hundred fifty-eight graduates,
One hundred-eighty graves.
The killing was easy;
The saving less so.

50th Annual Family Reunion

The old ones seemed bewildered
As they walked among their children
And their children's children
Wondering what they had wrought
Upon themselves and the world

Mario and Crew

i.

If you say,
They seem to be trying to stay in time.
You are mistaken.

Listen closely, watch with wonder
As Mario and crew ply their hoes;
In a short while you will know
There is no trying, nor seeming in the matter,
Only a natural rhythm of rasp and click,
Sound of steel striking stone and soil,
The cadence of their work.

ii

Morning sun rises,
Mario and crew climb
Out of the stripped down
'63' International Travelall,
Grab hoes and water jugs;
Little needs to be said,
For they know their work.
Mario knows the crew:

Skill, strength, stamina
Of each compadre.
He surveys the field,
Judges the pace needed
To cleanse it of weeds,
Disease and excess.
Without fail when
The old Travelall returns
Roaring, and trailing a plume
Of dust and oily exhaust,
The last licks of their hoes
Will be heard in the field--
The job completed.

iii

Mario and crew pray
Before the heat of the day
Begins to darken the fabric
Of their shirts with sweat;
By day's end their backs
Are as wet as the day
They crossed the Rio Grande
On their migration north
To labor and provide for tables
Back home in Mexico
And here in Pennsylvania --
Their work, communion.

iv

Cultivating the strawberry field
For only a half hour, they already
Lead my best pace by twenty yards.
I stop, lean on my hoe
To admire their silhouettes
Against the sunrise,
A synchronization of motion and sound.
I know the gap between us
Will only increase as the day progresses;
And they, smiling in good humor
Will join me in finishing my rows
Before they return home to rest.

v

Today Mario and his crew tend the strawberry fields
That must be cleaned of weeds that obstruct
Thoreau-inspired suburbanites who fancy a half hour
Of Pick-Your-Own as a day's labor worthy
Of their short cake and whipped cream.

vi

Thistle and dandelion
Cultivated in coupling
Of movement and sound...
A row becomes rows,
Rows become acres,
Acres a day's work.

Insomnia

i.

Your knock on my door
Imperceptible then
Echoes loudly in my heart
This sleepless night.

ii.

Possibly
Only a dream
That egret
Sitting frozen
On the bedpost
In the middle of the night

For Rent

Women who tried
To love him
Found a faded, stained
For Rent sign
On his heart,
Suggesting the rate
Cheap, even negotiable;
Though mostly,
At month's end,
Or maybe two,
They would
One night, quietly
Pack up, sneak out,
No risk, no pursuit,
No hard feelings,
Simply, business as usual,
Steady stream of renters
Willing to put up
With discomfort:
Lack of heat,
Faulty plumbing...
        for a while.

Frederick
      (September 12, 2016)

A small box

On the top shelf

Looks down upon them.

Within,

A bonnet, a gown

Barely worn,

Innocent of stain, ethereal,

Gently folded and lain

By weeping hands.

Within,

An icon

On shroud white,

Barely discernible toes,

Thin arch, tiny heel--

A footprint,

His.

Within,

An urn,

Unopened,

Round, soft blue,

Cradled in wanting hands.

Within,

      Within

Remains

All that was precious,

Consecrated by their love.

Silent Worship

Apparently,
The questioner considered
Sitting quietly and expectantly
A tedious business,
And such an hour spent
An approximation
Of eternal damnation.

My reply:
Once while kneeling
And toiling quietly
Among the lilies and foxglove
I sensed a perfect humming.
Turning my head
I found myself
Beak to beak
With a ruby-throat,
The perfect hummer.

Over the years, I spent
Countless hours quietly toiling,
Seeking another encounter.
My success matters not,
For both the garden and I
Benefit from the effort.

Last Day

Delete, delete, delete
Computer-scrubbed
Artifacts lost with a touch.

Piles of strata mucked
From an academic stall,

A life's work
Graded for the final
Time—recycle or trash?

Bookcases empty, treasures
Acquired one by one, now
Tossed into boxes,
Left on tables for passersby

Only the corkboard stands
Between memory and oblivion

Left behind:

Three posters, one poem
That a heart cannot remove.

Harvest

A rusty chain link fence surrounds this garden,

Porous, it does not imprison

Nor exclude as might stone;

The gate swings freely, admits all

But want to our side.

Translucent figures of another time,

From other places, wander here

In bibbed overalls and dusty fedora,

Flowered bonnets, cotton dresses,

Hems lifted lightly by a summer breeze.

The old ones share quiet joy

Found in patient sowing,

Cultivating the future…

The harvest of their work.

Acknowledgements

I am grateful for the invaluable support and nurturance I have received from my writing groups: Renshi Poets, The Watershed Writers Block Party, and Saturdays at The Bridge. Grateful acknowledgement is made to the editors of the following publications in which these poems first appeared, [some in different versions]:

"Jubilee"- *North/South Appalachia*

"Centered"- *The Watershed Journal*

"Risk"- *The Bridge Literary Arts Journal*

"Helix"- *The Watershed Journal*

"Leave-taking"- *The Bridge Literary Arts Journal*

"The Milking"- *The Watershed Journal*

"Shrug"- *The Watershed Journal*

"Rows"- *The Watershed Journal*

"Harvest"- *The Bridge Literary Arts Journal*

"Compassion: A Missed Opportunity"- *Friends Journal*

"Silent Worship"- *Friends Journal*

"Last Day"- *Tobeco*

"Cautionary Note"- *Tobeco*

Covers: My sincere gratitude to Susan Hadden for the cover sketches that capture the satisfied lean on a hoe after a day's work well done and the eager thrust of a spade to turn the soil for planting.

About the Author

A native Pennsylvanian, Wayne H. Swanger, has lived the past ten years in the northwest region of the state, much of which has been designated as the Pennsylvania Wilds. Many of the poems in *Fields of His Heart* germinated during walks under the towering hemlocks and white pines in Cook Forest; while floating on the Clarion River, a national scenic waterway; when snowshoeing or hiking on one of the myriad stretches of public ground in the area; and while simply tending his small orchard and garden. He goes afield with his wife, Mary and devoted English springer spaniel, Omega. His two sons, daughters-in-law and grandson reside in the Twin Cities.

Swanger's poetry has been published in *Friends Journal* and regional outlets including *The Watershed Journal*, *The Bridge Literary and Arts Journal* and Clarion University's *Tobeco*.

www.ingramcontent.com/pod-product-compliance
Lightning Source LLC
Chambersburg PA
CBHW072047040426
42447CB00012BB/3053